What Every Teacher Should Know About How Students Think:

A Survival Guide for Adults

Peter C. Ellsworth, M.S.T.
University of Wyoming
Laramie, Wyoming

and

Vincent G. Sindt, M.S.
University of Wyoming
Laramie, Wyoming

Thinking Publications
Eau Claire, Wisconsin

Library of Congress Cataloging-in-Publication Data

Ellsworth, Peter C.
    What every teacher should know about how students think : a survival guide for adults / Peter C. Ellsworth and Vincent G. Sindt.
        p.   cm.
    Rev. ed. of: Listening to your students think. 1984.
    Includes bibliographical references.
    ISBN 0-930599-74-8
    1. Cognition in children—United States. 2. School children—United States—Psychology. 3. Thought and thinking—Study and teaching—United States. I. Sindt, Vincent G. II. Ellsworth, Peter C. Listening to your students think. III. Title.
LB1062.E43   1992
370.15'2—dc20   91-42559
                                                                     CIP

01   00   99   98   97   96   95   94   10   9   8   7   6   5   4   3   2

Cover Design: Kris Madsen, Lines and Designs

Portions of this book were published in a previous edition of this work titled *Listening to Your Students Think: A Forgotten Fundamental in Education* (1984).

Printed in the United States of America

A Division of McKinley Companies, Inc.

P.O. Box 163
Eau Claire, WI 54702-0163
1-715-832-2488
FAX 1-715-832-9082

Table of Contents

Foreword

Interest in developing programs for teaching thinking skills has proliferated in the last decade. Apparent dissatisfaction with children's academic performance on tests and in classrooms, as well as the underlying anxiety created by the knowledge explosion, have required readjustment of educational programs. The proliferation of programs for teaching thinking reflects the search to discover the most productive ways to teach children how to discover and to solve problems, and how to think critically about solutions. These programs may be embedded in any one or more of the traditional academic disciplines (e.g., science, social science, literature, etc.). However, to enable children to become competent in these skills requires a competent teaching cadre. This may require retraining teachers by providing them the opportunities to reflect on their own teaching skills and to evaluate the degree to which their actions contribute to meeting these newly created demands on the school system. The time is right for articulating the focus on teaching as the necessary activity to enhance children's thinking.

Many programs are available, ranging from those which can be depicted as mechanistic skill approaches, wherein children and teachers are viewed almost as robots, to the more humanistic approach, which, while maintaining similar goals, attempts to achieve these goals by respecting the integrity of the person, whether the teacher or a student. The program described in this volume has embedded the values of respect for the person while at the same time providing an approach which attempts to facilitate individuals' fulfilling their intellectual, social, and emotional potential in the classroom environment. These values provide a fertile base on which to build so that children will emerge as thinkers and at the same time have a positive sense of themselves. After all, the human being is not compartmentalized into separate and isolated components, but rather functions as an organized, developing whole. Intellectual development occurs in this holistic context, and it is through attention to the unitary nature of the person that the intellectual objectives will be met. The objectives described, however well meaning in the abstract, have to be realized in the context of a practical world. This practical aspect is well articulated in this volume by Pete Ellsworth and Vince Sindt. They provide a humanistic orientation which should enable educators and their students to create a stimulating learning environment, yielding in the long run not "super babies" and not expert memorizers, but highly competent individuals who find learning and thinking exciting.

Irving E. Sigel
Educational Testing Service
Princeton, New Jersey

Acknowledgments

We have spent so much time discussing these ideas between ourselves and with our friends and colleagues over the years that we have long since lost track of which ideas were "Vince's," which were "Pete's," and which ones came from someone else. We don't care about which ones were ours, but we do wish we could be more accurate in crediting others for their contributions. Since that is not possible, we would at least like to give them our thanks, and hope that as they read and see evidence of their ideas, it will be enough to know that they made a difference.

We do want to give a very special thanks to Irving Sigel. Among the things we appreciate about him are these:

1. He is a distinguished researcher who cares in a deep and personal way about translating the results of research into the real world of teachers and kids.

2. He is a "nurturer" of people like ourselves, of questionable reputation (and character) whose primary concern is implementing these ideas in classrooms. At times we have wondered if we were on the right track, or whether the Wyoming winters had finally gotten to us. His willingness to drop everything and take time to talk about our questions and ideas has made a big difference. If we succeed in stimulating your interest to a point where you would like to do more reading on the subject, we can't think of a better place to start than with his work. In

particular, we have found three of his books, *Cognitive Development from Childhood to Adolescence: A Constructivist Perspective* (Sigel and Cocking, 1977), *Educating the Young Thinker: Classroom Strategies for Cognitive Growth* (Copple, Sigel, and Saunders, 1979), and *New Directions in Piagetian Theory and Practice* (Sigel, Brodzinsky, and Golnikoff, 1981), to be most helpful. (See the "Selected Resources" section for details.) We have been particularly impressed by his Distancing Hypothesis. When you begin to work on the problem of how to create cognitive disequilibrium in students, and how to ask questions, we suspect that you will find his writings on "distancing" to be of great value.

We also thank Dr. Joseph Stepans of the University of Wyoming for sharing his enlightening student interviews with us.

Pete Ellsworth
Vince Sindt

Chapter One

Assumptions, Definitions, and Rationale

Art Linkletter made a fortune doing it. Parents love to share stories about it. Many teachers promise some day to write a book about it. "It" in this case is the process of listening to all those cute and crazy things kids say. For example, the following exchange took place between a teacher and a 7-year-old student:

Teacher: "What is night?"

Student: "When it gets dark and the moon and stars come out."

Teacher: "Why does it get dark at night?"

Student: "Because you can't sleep in the daytime."

Teacher: "Where does the darkness come from?"

Student: "Black paper."

Teacher: "What is day?"

Student: "White paper . . . and when the sky is clear it's blue paper."

Teacher: "What makes day turn to night?"

Student: "They change the paper."

Kids do indeed say the darndest things, and it is great fun to listen to them. It is, however, a good deal more than that. The things they say, and in particular the way they answer questions, can tell us a great deal about how they think, if we learn how to listen.

The issue of teaching "thinking skills" continues to be a hot topic in the world of education. We find

1

Why can you hear the ocean in a seashell?

ourselves fascinated by the fact that much of the discussion is focused on how adults think and is being carried on as if kids were just small adults. They are not. They have their own view of the world, they think in ways that are different from adults, and if we are going to help them develop a more "grown up" way of thinking, we must become skilled at understanding what is really going on when they say "the darndest things." For example, the skilled listener can learn a great deal about how the child in the example thinks about the world, and what types of instruction are and are not appropriate for that child. That is what this little book is about. As you proceed, you will also become acquainted with a character named Quincy the Question Mark. There is no direct relationship between Quincy's question and the text of the book, but we think that both will give you a chance to do some thinking.

An assumption which underlies our work is that one learns better by "doing" than by reading. We therefore resisted writing this document. What caused us to change our minds was the fact that we have had so many requests from people who have attended our workshops for something to take with them which would allow for some focused reflection on the content of the workshop after we had left. We are not sure about the value of this document for those of you who have not attended the workshop . . . perhaps it will encourage you to join us sometime.

ASSUMPTIONS

The assumptions upon which we shall proceed are:

1. Thinking is a basic skill; in fact, it is the central purpose of education.

2. We know a great deal about how to teach kids to think, but . . .

3. For the last decade we have devoted so little time to teaching kids to think, that we have all but forgotten how it is done.

4. There are some powerful reasons for Assumption 3 which must be understood, so that we do not allow them to get in our way.

5. Schools are organized in such a way as to make the teaching of thinking skills more difficult than need be, but the problem with our schools is the way they are organized and *not* the people who work in them.

Thinking is a basic skill; in fact, it is the central purpose of education.

WHAT WE MEAN BY THINKING

Later in this document we will replace this definition with one that is more precise and functional, but for our present purposes, we will define thinking in an operational way by describing some abilities of a student who can "think." Specifically, that student should be able to:

1. understand the concepts we are trying to teach, and

2. approach the task of understanding concepts with enthusiasm.

We suspect that the importance of students being able to understand concepts is obvious, but we should add that by "understand" we mean students are able to apply the concept to a new situation—one they have never seen before—rather than simply memorizing the definition of the concept or the formula for solving problems.

How could a boy's grandfather be only six years older than the boy's father?

This definition may appear limited when compared to more scholarly definitions, such as those presented in ASCD's excellent summary, *Dimensions of Thinking* (Marzano, Brandt, Hughes, Jones, Rankin, and Suhor, 1988), but it has been functional for us because it directly addresses what teachers care about when they teach content. We think that of the more scholarly definitions, ours is most closely tied to

Sigel's ideas of "representational competence" (Sigel and Cocking, 1977).

Another reason why the definition is not as limited as it may appear is that many of the concepts which we ask students to understand are abstract, complex, and involve multiple interacting variables, trends, theories, and probabilities where one clear answer is not evident. True understanding of these concepts requires the development of the same mental structures which are described later as we expand our definition of "thinking."

We also want to emphasize the fact that we understand the "thinking" dimension of a student is only one dimension of that person. We are not talking about the social dimension, the physical dimension, the emotional dimension, the sexual dimension, or any of the others which combine to make up the whole person. We understand the importance of these dimensions, but we are at this time only interested in the cognitive dimension because it is this which we, as educators, are expected to affect the most.

WHY WE SHOULD PROCEED

The individual with developed *rational* powers can share deeply in the freedoms his society offers and can contribute most to the preservation of those freedoms. At the same time, she/he will have the best chance of understanding and contributing to the great events of his/her time. And the society which best develops the rational potentials of its people, along with their intuitive and aesthetic capabilities, will have the best chance of flourishing in the future. To help every person develop those powers is therefore a profoundly important objective and one which increases in importance with the passage of time. By

The society which best develops the rational potentials of its people, along with their intuitive and aesthetic capabilities, will have the best chance of flourishing in the future.

pursuing this objective, the school can enhance spiritual and aesthetic values and the other cardinal purposes which it has traditionally served and must continue to serve. The purpose which runs through and strengthens all other educational purposes, the common thread of education, is the development of the ability to think. (Educational Policies Commission, 1963)

These words were written by the Educational Policies Commission of the National Education Association and the American Association of School Administrators three decades ago, and they remain an eloquent statement of the philosophy which guides this document. As we write, the country continues to reflect upon the nature of school and to criticize the performance of our schools and our students. The first edition of this volume was published shortly after the release of the report of the National Commission on Excellence in Education in 1983, which was the first of a series of studies whose common theme has been that our nation's schools are not adequately preparing students to deal with the world as it will exist in the 21st century. (More recent examples include reports by Mullis and Jenkins [1988]; Mullis, Owen, and Phillips [1990]; and Mullis, Dossey, Owen, and Phillips [1991]). Most states and school districts are developing and implementing plans in reaction to the criticism in these studies, and a key component of these plans continues to be a strong emphasis on getting "back to the basics." It fascinates us that for all the sound and fury this issue has generated, no one of prominence is successfully making the point that the "back to the basics" movement has been the major focus of activity in our school for 20 years now. There have been other issues to be sure, including the education of the handicapped and gifted and talented, bilingual education, and the introduction of the microcomputer. None of these, however, has commanded the time, effort, or attention that has been devoted to the basic skills. We believe that there are not many accidents in this world; so if we have devoted two entire decades to working on the basic skills and no one noticed, we would be well advised to ask, "Why?"

We believe at least part of the reason is that we have been on the wrong track. The problem is that we have limited our definition of basic skills to the so-called "three R's." We have treated reading, writing, and arithmetic as if they exist and operate in a vacuum. They do not. They have a purpose: They are tools for thinking. It is true that we read for pleasure, but we also read to learn and to locate information which can support or disprove our ideas. We write to communicate our thoughts about things, and we do some of our best thinking when forced to focus our thoughts by writing them down. Arithmetic is a tool for thinking about quantities and quantitative processes.

3

Why is it so quiet after a snowstorm?

Unfortunately, we have taught these skills as if they were an end in themselves, rather than a means to an end. We should not be surprised, therefore, when achievement test scores, a national report summarizing

20 years of educational progress (Mullis et al., 1990), and our own observations show that as we have shifted our emphasis from "thinking" to the mechanics of the three R's, our students' ability to think has declined. A basic skills program which does not include a "thinking skills" component produces only superficial growth in problem-solving abilities.

The facts are that persons who are not able to understand abstract concepts such as nationalism, density, or ratio and proportion are not going to be able to read or write about those concepts with under-standing—no matter how much time they have spent on phonics or spelling, or how many vocabulary words they have memorized. They are also not going to be able to make calculations related to the concept, no matter how many pages of practice problems they have done. On a more positive note, Shepard (1989) points out that students given instruction aimed at conceptual understanding do better on skills tests than students drilled on the skills directly. In one of our favorite examples, Worsham and Austin (1983) report a study in which 40 percent of a secondary language arts curriculum was replaced with a think-ing skills program, and the result was a 42-point increase in the verbal portion of the Stanford Achievement Test (Madden et al., 1973).

The good news about the recent criticism of public education is that *for the first time in a decade, "think-ing" is being recognized as one of the basics.* We now have an opportunity to attack the problem from a direc-tion that has a reasonable chance of success. That direc-tion is to recognize that our central purpose in educa-tion is to teach kids to "think"; while the three R's are important, they are only a means to an end, not an end

A basic skills program which does not include a "thinking skills" component produces only superficial growth in problem-solving abilities.

in themselves. We agree with the observation that claiming that the three R's constitute education is like claiming that a knife, fork, and spoon constitute dinner.

A SHIFT IN FOCUS

Once we educators make the decision to work on teaching kids to think, we need to make a change in the way we think about the business of teaching. A friend of ours once described that shift as moving from a "focus on teaching to a focus on learning." We freely admit that, as it stands, this looks simplistic, but it has become clear to us that this really is a very powerful idea. Therefore, we wish to invest some time to add meaning to those words. Consider the following: *If a student is working on but cannot master an objective, then one of two things must be true: Either the instruction was not effective, or the objective was not appropriate for that student in the first place.*

As we work with educators, we find the idea that different objectives might be appropriate or inappropriate for different students is almost never considered, and the question of appropriateness is one example of what we mean by a shift to a focus on learning. Earlier in this chapter, one of the organizational problems to which we referred in Assumption 5 is the fact that because we are so focused on teaching rather than learning, we are driving ourselves and the kids crazy by trying to teach objectives for which they are not yet ready. Instead of devoting ourselves to providing the kinds of experiences which will lead to readiness, we develop elaborate "mastery" programs which kids can only survive by memorizing. We then give them a test which only measures their ability to

If a student is working on but cannot master an objective, then one of two things must be true: Either the instruction was not effective, or the objective was not appropriate for that student in the first place.

memorize, and we proceed, convinced that the students have "mastered" the concept.

When the two of us first began teaching, we assumed that all, or at least most, of our students were fully capable of understanding the concepts we were trying to teach. Our jobs, as we understood them,

If hot air rises, why does the snow stay on the tops of mountains?

were to find a combination of tricks which fell within the limits of time, money, and good sense and which would cause understanding to be achieved. In most cases, this involved trying to provide a clear definition of the concept, a variety of illustrative examples, and a test to find out how well the students had mastered the concept, and then to move on to the next concept. Notice, please, that we did not think about the test as indicating how well we had mastered teaching the concept. We will also confess that at that point we had not thought much about what we meant by "understanding," and as a result, most of our tests could be passed by a student who was willing to take the time to memorize a certain body of information. Finally, we will admit that we discovered there were many concepts which we had not understood until we tried to teach them to others, even though we did well in college courses covering these concepts. What we did not understand, and what no one told us, was that because most of those concepts were abstract and complex, they were, *by definition,* beyond the abilities of many of our students to understand. Keep in mind that by "understand" we mean the ability to apply the concept to a brand new situation, not the ability to memorize facts and formulas. The model we used looked something like this:

Model #1

Step 1: Decide, or be told, to teach a concept.

Step 2: Tell the students about the concept and provide some examples.

Step 3: Give a test to find out how they did.

We will say more about this later, but in place of this model we propose the following:

Model #2

Step 1: Identify the concepts which are important enough to be included in your curriculum.

Step 2: Identify the thinking abilities of your students.

Step 3: Analyze your curriculum to determine the type of thinking it requires. (We will describe some types of thinking later.)

Step 4: Develop, or find, instructional activities which are appropriate for the cognitive development of your students and "learning cycles" for the concepts you have decided to teach.

Step 5: Assess student understanding of the concept to determine how well your strategies worked and what to do next (i.e., post-assessment).

We find, as did Dr. Goodlad (1984), that the first model describes what goes on in most classrooms and exemplifies what we mean by a focus on teaching. The second model illustrates what we mean by a focus on learning.

One problem with the second model is the fact that most of us do not have a clear understanding of how our students think, and without that understanding, it is not possible to make the model work. Unfortunately, helping us to understand how our students think has not been a very high priority for our teacher-training institutions, our state departments of education, or our local school districts. It is interesting to speculate about how the world of education would change if our teacher-training institutions made sure that prospective teachers understood (not memorized and passed the test as in Model #1) how students think and how to design instruction that is appropriate for how they think and learn. What if state departments of education threw out all of their other requirements and replaced them with one which required prospective teachers to be able to identify the cognitive characteristics of their students and plan appropriate instruction based upon that identification? Suppose that school districts recognized that their staffs have been poorly served in this area and made a commitment to provide in-service. It appears to us that local school districts are moving faster in this area than are departments of education or colleges and universities, but because they do not understand how children think, many of these districts are devoting their resources to programs which teach for mastery rather than developing understanding as we have defined it. In the next section, we will report what we know about this subject.

HOW CHILDREN THINK

To understand how kids think, we need to return to the wonderful world of developmental psychology. We say "return" on purpose, because we know that almost all of you, or at least those of you who are educators, passed an education course which "covered" this material at some point in your career. We will bet that the course you passed followed Model #1.

A basic principle of developmental psychology is that intellectual development is not a linear process. As children develop cognitively, they go through distinct, discrete periods. These periods are qualitatively different from one another and are passed through in a specific order. The periods which apply to most school-age children are called "preoperational," "concrete," and "formal." The importance of understanding the periods lies in the fact that if a student is functioning at one stage and is presented with a problem or an idea which requires thinking at a higher stage, the student will not be able to solve the problem or understand the idea. We have included the ages which are used in most textbooks on human development, but we caution you that most of your students will not have reached the level you would expect at a given age.

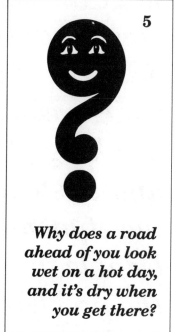

5

Why does a road ahead of you look wet on a hot day, and it's dry when you get there?

17

If a student is functioning at one stage and is presented with a problem or an idea which requires thinking at a higher stage, the student will not be able to solve the problem or understand the idea.

The Preoperational Learner
(Ages 2–7 Years)

The following are characteristics of a child in the preoperational period:

1. *Reasoning is not based upon accepted adult logic.* Consider the question, "Where does the wind go on a calm day?"—a perfectly logical question to an adult. A perfectly logical answer to a preoperational child might be, "It goes to three little towns, then to Sheridan, and then to Cheyenne."

2. *Thinking is not reversible.* For example, while a child is watching you, take a tube and place a red block, a blue block, and a green block in it in order. Turn the tube over and ask the child to tell you the order in which the blocks will come out. To be able to tell the order correctly requires the child to mentally reverse the order in which the blocks were placed in the tube. A preoperational child will not be able to perform this task (Sigel and Cocking, 1977). Another example of this characteristic is that a child can be walked to school, but that same child during this learning phase will not be able to reverse the process and find the way home. Students must have developed the skill of reversibility to understand the process of subtraction.

3. *Thought is limited to only what is being acted upon.* This characteristic leads to responses such as the one in paragraph 1 above. Thus, a child leaving a snowball on the sidewalk returns to find a puddle of water, yet will see no relationship between the snowball and the water.

19

4. *Thinking and behavior are egocentric.* All thinking and events are evaluated as the child sees them, and the child believes that everyone thinks and feels as he or she does.

5. *Attention centers upon only one detail of an event, situation, or problem.* For example, a child may believe that "Mommy" is older than grandmother because "Mommy" is bigger. The child focuses only on the detail of size.

6. *There is no conservation of number, substance, length, area, or time.* The child does not recognize that the characteristics of objects, events, and situations remain the same in spite of perceived external changes. The classic example involves showing a child two identical pieces of clay. One of the pieces is then flattened into the shape of a pancake. The nonconserving child will not believe that the two pieces still weigh the same.

The Concrete Learner (Ages 7–11 Years)

Skills Which a Concrete Learner Has Mastered

1. *Classification*—classifies and generalizes on the basis of observable characteristics.

2. *Conservation*—recognizes that the characteristics of objects, events, or situations remain the same in spite of perceived external changes.

3. *Serial ordering*—arranges in order a set of objects, events, or situations according to an observable characteristic and establishes a one-to-one relationship between two observable sets.

4. *Reversibility*—mentally invents a sequence of steps to return from the final condition of a procedure to its initial condition.

Capabilities of a Concrete Learner

1. Understands concepts and simple hypotheses that make direct reference to familiar actions and objects.

2. Follows step-by-step instructions, as in a recipe, provided each step is completely specified.

3. Relates one's viewpoint to those of others in simple situations.

Limitations of a Concrete Learner

1. Needs to refer to familiar actions, objects, and observable properties.

2. Uses classification, conservation, and serial ordering skills, and establishes one-to-one correspondence only in relation to familiar actions, objects, and observable properties.

3. Needs step-by-step instructions to perform a lengthy procedure.

4. Lacks awareness of own reasoning. Does not recognize inconsistencies among various statements or contradictions of statements with other known facts.

5. Recognizes "black and white areas" but doesn't understand or acknowledge the possibility of "grey areas" in a problem or situation. Thinking is absolute.

The Formal Learner (Ages 11 and Older)

Skills Which a Formal Learner Has Mastered

1. *Theoretical reasoning*—applies multiple classification, conservation logic, serial ordering, and other reasoning skills to relationships and properties which are not easily observable.

21

2. *Combinatorial reasoning*—systematically considers all conceivable relations of creative, experimental, or theoretical conditions, even though some may not be "practical."

3. *Isolation and control of variables*—identifies the variables and designs tests that control all the variables except the one being investigated.

4. *Proportional logic*—recognizes when a ratio must be used to solve a problem.

5. *Probabilistic reasoning*—recognizes that natural events are probabilistic in character, and that conclusions or explanations are often based on probability and chance rather than certainty.

6. *Correlational reasoning*—identifies relationships between two situations, events, or variables and at advanced levels can quantify the strength of the relationship. Understands that exceptions do not necessarily negate the relationship.

Capabilities of a Formal Learner

1. Reasons with concepts, relationships, abstract properties, axioms, and theories.

2. Uses symbols to express ideas.

3. Applies logical skills such as combinatorial reasoning, classification, conservation, serial ordering, and proportional reasoning in abstract modes of thought.

4. Plans lengthy procedures to attain given goals.

5. Is aware and critical of his or her own reasoning process and actively checks the validity of conclusions by appealing to other information.

This list is not 100 percent complete and has been interpreted in different ways by different scholars. It should, however, provide enough information to give a clear view of the differences between periods. For an interesting alternative definition of the intellectual stages of development, see the list of formal skills in *The Arlin Test of Formal Reasoning* (Arlin, 1984).

A Simplified Summary of Thinking Skill Development

For the purpose of this document, the preceding information can be simplified in the following way:

- Preoperational thinkers have a logical view of the world which makes perfect sense to them but has little, if anything, to do with the type of logic expected from students in school. We can "train" them to say that a clay ball still weighs the same when we smash it into a pancake, but if they are not able to conserve weight they won't believe it, and they will see the whole exercise as further evidence that teachers lie to little kids.

- Concrete learners are logical in the adult sense, but can only think logically about things which they can experience directly with their senses. Ideas or concepts which involve abstractions or complexities are beyond them. Again, they can memorize the words or formulas, but they do not understand them.

- Only when (and if) students reach the formal level are they truly able to understand abstract and complex ideas, concepts, and processes such as democracy, the free enterprise system, genetics, or any of the formal concepts which we try to teach on a daily basis.

23

We are not being negative when we say that from an instructional point of view, the interesting thing about nonformal thinkers is what they cannot do; by definition, what they cannot do is understand concepts, ideas, or processes which require formal thought. Table 1.1 summarizes key characteristics at each level of thinking.

Skilled problem solvers have the mental structuring of formal operations but are able to move freely

Table 1.1: Key Characteristics

Preoperational

- Bases prelogical reasoning on perceptions of the moment
  - irreversible and nonconserving thought
- Thinks egocentrically
- Centers attention on single detail
- Lacks adult logic and reasoning

Concrete

- Bases logical reasoning on "observable" properties or "familiar" actions, objects, events
  - reversible thought
  - conserves, classifies, orders, and generalizes to familiar or observable situations
- Takes others' points of view
- Follows step-by-step, specific instructions
- Reasons but is unaware of own reasoning and contradictions

Formal

- Applies logical reasoning to abstract concepts, relationships, properties, theories
  - applies reasoning to conservation, classification, ordering, proportions, probability for nonobserved and unfamiliar situations
- Uses symbols to express own ideas and ideas of others
- Plans and follows lengthy procedures to attain goal
- Is aware and critical of own reasoning; checks validity

between formal and concrete reasoning. They can employ both in solving their problems. Some of our colleagues operate well with formal reasoning, but seem to be lacking common sense. This is often the inability to move back to concrete thinking when necessary.

REVISED DEFINITIONS

Earlier, we promised to expand our definition of thinking skills. From here on:

1. When we talk about thinking skills, we are talking about the characteristics and relationships among preoperational, concrete, and formal thought.

2. When we talk about higher-level thinking skills, we are talking about the characteristics of formal thought.

3. When we talk about appropriateness and shifting from a focus on teaching to a focus on learning, we are talking about objectives which are consistent with the cognitive level of the student and instruction which will help that student to develop the characteristics of formal thought.

6

You can touch and move only one glass. Change the line so that no empty glass is next to another empty one and no full glass is next to a full one.

25

The problem with schools is the way they are organized, not the people who work in them.

Chapter Two

The Problem

POOR SCHOOL ORGANIZATION

One of our initial assumptions was that the problem with schools is the way they are organized, not the people who work in them. One example of this is the fact that schools are organized as if children all move from the preoperational level to the concrete level during the summer between kindergarten and first grade, and as if they all become formal thinkers before they enter junior high school. Table 2.1 describes what you can expect to find if you assess the cognitive levels of your students (Epstein, 1979). To use the table, read down the left-hand column until you find the age of the children you teach, then read across the table to determine the percentage of students operating at each level. "Onset" and "mature" refer to the relative consistency observed in students when solving problems. For example, upon entry into the concrete period, behaviors from the preoperational period also continue; this is the onset stage of concrete operations. As behaviors become more integrated and concrete reasoning is consistently demonstrated, the student is considered "mature." The same scenario is repeated when making the transition into formal operations.

Table 2.1: Cognitive Levels

AGE (YRS.)	PREOPERA-TIONAL	CONCRETE ONSET	CONCRETE MATURE	FORMAL ONSET	FORMAL MATURE
5	85	15			
6	60	35	5		
7	35	55	10		
8	25	55	20		
9	15	55	30		
10	12	52	35	1	
11	6	49	40	5	
12	5	32	51	12	
13	2	34	44	14	6
14	1	32	43	15	9
15	1	14	53	19	13
16	1	15	54	17	13
17	3	19	47	19	12
18	1	15	50	15	19

H.J. Epstein. (1979). Cognitive growth and development, *Colorado Journal of Educational Research, 19*(1), pp. 4–5.

A more recent study by Renner and Marek (1988) shows similar results. The study used 811 students in grades 10 through 12. Each student had three opportunities to demonstrate complete formal thought. Formal thought demonstrations were found 43 percent of the time; concrete thought demonstrations were found 57 percent of the time.

Table 2.1, we hope, illustrates the mess we get ourselves into by focusing on teaching rather than learning. Hundreds of thousands of educators have devoted countless millions of hours developing and implementing curricula without ever asking the question of whether what they are trying to do is appropriate for their students. If you think for a minute about the characteristics of formal thought and then look at the objectives, activities, and tests in your curriculum, you will see that as early as the primary grades, children are being asked to perform tasks which require formal thought. But the data show that less than 20 percent of our nation's 18-year-olds have reached that level. For nearly two decades, we have been scaring ourselves to death with achievement test scores, but hardly anyone has paid attention to what appears to us to be a far more serious problem: our failure to help children develop the higher-level thinking skills of formal thought. Our solution has been to treat the symptoms instead of the cause. We are frequently reminded of the old line about rearranging the deck chairs on the Titanic.

Can you arrange four nines (9,9,9,9) to total 100? You can use each nine only once.

CONFUSING MEMORIZATION AND UNDERSTANDING

An obvious question at this point is that if a curriculum demands formal thought, and less than 20 percent of our 18-year-olds think at that level, how is

For nearly two decades, we have been scaring ourselves to death with achievement test scores, but hardly anyone has paid attention to a far more serious problem: our failure to help children develop the higher-level thinking skills of formal thought.

it possible for more than 20 percent of our students to graduate? The answer, of course, is that we don't require them to understand the curriculum. Instead, we require them to memorize and repeat to us a massive collection of words and mathematical tricks. We also develop in them a sophisticated ability to manipulate concrete "crutches" which allow them to solve problems so long as there are no new, unknown situations or variables involved. Their ability to use these crutches hides from us, and from them, their lack of real understanding. If they are able to accomplish this memorization task, we certify them as competent and graduate them. We do not wish to suggest that there

Why did my hand get cold when I dropped alcohol on it?

is no value in memory, for in fact it is an important part of the learning process. The point is that while it is important, memorizing is different from understanding and should not be used as an indicator of understanding. One problem with confusing memory and understanding is illustrated on the following page by Figure 2.1 (United States Forest Service, 1972).

As Figure 2.1 demonstrates, we retain attitudes at a 100 percent level after a year, while retaining thinking skills and processes at an 80 percent level. On the other hand, factual material which must be memorized is retained at a level of only 35 percent after three months. We invite you to close your eyes for a moment and speculate as to the percentage of time devoted to the memorization of factual material in our schools, grades K through 12, nationwide. If you came up with a figure in the 75–85 percent range, your guess would coincide with the findings of the Goodlad

Figure 2.1
Percentage of Useful Information Retained Assuming 100% Original Effectiveness

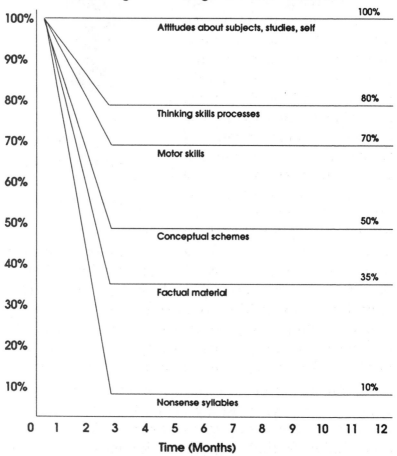

United States Forest Service. (1972). *Environmental Education for Teachers and Research People.* Washington, DC: U.S. Department of Agriculture, p.1.

Because we have not based our curricula or instruction on what we know about how children think and learn, we have developed objectives and tried to teach concepts and processes which are beyond the abilities of our students.

study (1984). On the other hand, the amount of time devoted to thinking skills is less than 10 percent.

In an international airliner crash on the U.S.-Mexican border, where does the law say you must bury the survivors?

It turns out that we devote lots of time to developing attitudes, but not on purpose. We are very successful at teaching students that learning is boring. That may not be the attitude we wish to develop, but that is exactly what happens. We believe the reason it happens is that, either consciously or subconsciously, we know that the students are not ready for real understanding of the abstract concepts we are trying to teach. To avoid flunking them, we resort to memory-level activities and tests which they are able to do, but which are also nonproductive and boring.

To state the problem simply, it is that because we have not based our curricula or instruction on what we know about out how children think and learn, we have developed objectives and tried to teach concepts and processes which are beyond the abilities of our students. Because they are not able to understand, but are able to memorize, we have evolved an instructional system which devotes almost all of its time (which really means our time) to teaching students to memorize, and almost no time to developing their ability to think.

34

Chapter Three

The Solution

The good news in all of this is that the problem can be solved. We know how to develop thinking skills. The process involves:

- accepting the definition of "understanding," which requires that children be able to apply what they have learned to new, unfamiliar situations, and

- replacing instructional Model #1 with Model #2 (see page 15). The five steps of Model #2 are expanded below.

STEP #1—IDENTIFY THE CONCEPTS WHICH ARE IMPORTANT ENOUGH TO BE INCLUDED IN YOUR CURRICULUM

This is a decision you will have to make for yourself. The following information may be helpful.

- Which concepts you choose does not matter, because what you are really developing are the abilities to understand all concepts and enthusiasm for doing so. If you can't cover all the concepts you wish during the time you have with students, there is now a chance that they will have the interest and ability to learn other concepts on their own.

- Because it doesn't matter which concepts you cover, we would encourage you to choose the ones with which you are most familiar. The more you know about a concept, the more able you will be to ask helpful and thought-provoking questions.

- Developing children's understanding of concepts takes more time than forcing them to memorize, so you won't be able to "cover" as much material as you used to.

STEP #2—IDENTIFY THE THINKING ABILITIES OF YOUR STUDENTS

During this step, you learn to listen to your children thinking. For us, this is one of the most interesting parts of the process. The assessment process will provide you with the information you need to provide instruction which is appropriate for your students. However, especially if you are new to this process, you will find that this is also an excellent way to develop your own understanding of the concepts we are discussing. We found that we really did not understand terms such as "conservation of number" and "combinatorial logic" until we had actually done these activities with students. Before you begin, we should provide a few cautions:

1. First, and above all, for this process to work, students must feel free to express their thoughts openly. Therefore, it is absolutely essential that you *not* give them any clue, verbal

Developing children's understanding of concepts takes more time than forcing them to memorize, so you won't be able to "cover" as much material as you used to.

or otherwise, as to whether their answer is correct or not. The purpose of the assessment is to determine the level of cognitive development of the students, not to judge them. If any judgments are to be made, they should be of the instruction the students have had, not of the students themselves. If the students find out that they are going to be punished for not knowing the "right" answer, they will avoid participating, and the process will not work. -

2. Another reason for allowing students to express their thinking honestly is that all a correct answer tells you is that the student may have developed the cognitive structure. The interesting information comes from the students' explanation of their answers, especially incorrect ones. By analyzing the explanations of incorrect answers, you learn the most about how your students are thinking and what sorts of instructional interventions will be productive. Also, you may learn that what appeared to be an incorrect answer was actually a correct one. For example, we are occasionally told that the clay pancake weighs less than the ball because when we flattened it, we left some of the clay on our hands. Students who give this response are clearly conservers

10

How many animals did Adam take onto the Ark with him?

of substance even though their initial response appeared to be incorrect.

3. The best way to gain accurate information about the development of students is to conduct assessments by using the format of an individual interview. However, individual interviews are time consuming, and if they are not practical for you, there are assessment instruments available. We have developed "The Classroom Assessment of Student Reasoning" (Ellsworth and Sindt, 1991) for this purpose, but we also recommend *Piagetian Activities* (Copeland, 1988) for elementary students and *The Arlin Test of Formal Reasoning* (Arlin, 1984) for secondary students.

4. It will take some time and effort to become comfortable with the process. Keep in mind that as your understanding increases, the amount of time will decrease, and that the alternative is to proceed without the information, which is not a productive way to operate.

5. Finally, remember that as you become familiar with the process, you will get to the point where you begin to do it informally and intuitively. When you reach that point, it will be a natural and effortless part of your daily routine.

The following sections provide examples of the assessment process.

Conservation of Number

Arrange the setting so that the child is sitting across from you at a table. Place eight checkers of one color in a straight line with approximately one inch between them. The child is then given a group of chips of

These children have not yet developed concrete ability to conserve number, and to attempt to teach them arithmetic is going to be an exercise in futility for you and for them.

another color and is asked to place one of them opposite each of the ones in your line. Make sure that the child knows there is a one-to-one correspondence between the two lines of chips. Then say, "Watch what I do," and proceed to move your line of chips into a group or pile. Now ask, "Are there more chips in your line, are there the same number of chips in the line as in my pile, or are there more chips in my pile?" Allow the child to reply, then ask for an explanation of this answer. You may be surprised to discover that, especially in the primary grades, some children will believe that there are now more chips in the line, because it is "bigger." These children have not yet developed concrete ability to conserve number, and to attempt

11

If I'm standing on a bathroom scale and lift up one foot, will I get heavier, lighter, or stay the same?

to teach them arithmetic is going to be an exercise in futility for you and for them. They can memorize words, such as "five plus three equals eight," but it should be clear that they do not have a clue as to what those words mean.

This is an excellent example of why we insist that the definition of "understanding" which we are using is more sensible. The nonconserving child who had memorized the words could pass a "mastery" test which asked him or her to answer the question "5+3=?," but when confronted by the problem in a

Is my hat taller or wider?

new situation, would be unable to apply that knowledge. This is not to suggest that educators do nothing related to number with nonconserving children. Children's lack of cognitive development is a strong indication that their experiences with numbers and the links between numbers and their representations have had little meaning. Experiences with numbers that are meaningful should be provided, such as using hands-on manipulative materials (e.g., putting a flower in every vase).

Conservation of Weight (Substance)

Show the child two equal balls of clay and ask, "Do these balls of clay weigh the same?" The answer to this question must be "yes" before proceeding. Then say, "Watch what I am doing with this ball," and smash it into a pancake shape. Hold up the other ball and the pancake shape and ask, "Is there more clay in this ball, is there the same amount of clay in the two pieces, or is there more clay in this pancake?" Ask the child to explain his or her answer.

Again, you may be surprised to find that some children believe that by changing the shape, you have changed the amount, or the weight. These children will not be able to do anything but memorize when confronted with problems requiring these concepts, until they have developed the ability to conserve. We are not suggesting that teachers should avoid the idea of weight, but rather that it be presented in an exploratory, hands-on, engaging way, so as to help students develop the ability to conserve.

Conservation of Liquid (Volume)

Show the child two identical glasses containing equal amounts of colored liquid and ask, "If this is Kool-Aid® for a party, do we have exactly the same amount in each glass?" Make sure the answer is "yes" before proceeding. Say, "Watch what I do," and pour the liquid from one of the containers into a tall, thin one. Ask, "Does this shorter glass have more Kool-Aid® in it, do the two containers have the same amount, or does the tall glass have more Kool-Aid® in it?" Then ask for an explanation of the answer. Again, children who do not

13

Can you describe to me what thunder sounds like?

see that the amount stays the same in this situation will not be able to deal with the problems involving quarts, pints, liters, or other measures of liquid volume with any understanding, and will have to memorize. Once again, we believe that students' failure to develop this understanding is a reflection of a lack of meaningful experiences, and we encourage teachers to

43

explore these ideas with their students and help them to anchor the meaning to real experiences.

STEP #3—ANALYZE YOUR CURRICULUM TO DETERMINE THE TYPE OF THINKING IT REQUIRES

14

What comes next here?

A,B,C,D,E,___, ___, ___

A,B,A,C,A,___, ___, ___, ___, ___

A,D,G,J,M,___, ___, ___

O,T,T,F,F,___, ___, ___, ___

M,T,W,T,___, ___, ___

J,F,M,A,___, ___, ___

It is difficult to say much about this step without knowing what is actually in your curriculum, but the process is to look at each concept you are trying to teach and to ask questions such as these:

- Is the concept abstract or concrete?

- Which of the characteristics of concrete or formal thought must students possess to be able to understand this concept?

This task will be challenging at first, but as you become more familiar with these concepts, you will become more comfortable with the process.

Another important question to ask yourself about your objectives, your assignments, and your tests is, "Can students answer these questions or meet this objective by using memory, or is there something which they must understand and apply?" Additional questions in this analysis include considering the kind of information being taught, which can be classified as factual, procedural, or contextual. *Factual* information is defined as that which is known to exist or be true or have happened on the basis of actual experience or observation. *Procedural* information is taught when the learner must successfully complete a number of actions or thoughts in an invariant sequence in order to accomplish a task or master an objective. *Contextual* information provides the context or meaning for the facts and procedures.

15

My orange box almost collapsed when I sat on it. Will it hold as many oranges now?

An interesting analysis of your objectives can be carried out by developing a matrix which lists the level of knowledge (concrete or formal operational) on one axis, and the type of knowledge involved (factual, procedural, or contextual) on the other. Figure 3.1 illustrates this matrix. When this matrix is applied to many school district objective lists, educators are surprised to find out that they have far too many factual and procedural objectives and a distinct shortage of contextual ones. Even more concern is generated when people find a significant number of formal operational objectives when they know their students are using predominately concrete operations. For example, an economics unit requires comprehension of the complex relationships of supply and demand, and price requires formal thought and is probably ill-advised for elementary students.

Figure 3.1
Matrix That Can Be Applied
to Analysis of Educational Objectives

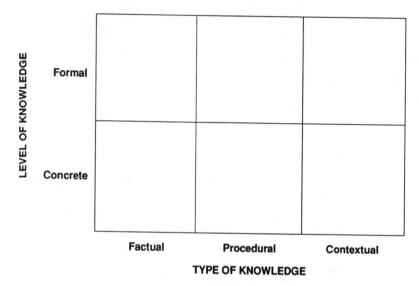

STEP #4—DEVELOP, OR FIND, INSTRUCTIONAL ACTIVITIES WHICH ARE APPROPRIATE FOR THE COGNITIVE DEVELOPMENT OF YOUR STUDENTS AND "LEARNING CYCLES" FOR THE CONCEPTS YOU HAVE DECIDED TO TEACH

In this step, we move from planning into actual instruction and begin to consider what types of teaching will (and will not) develop the thinking skills we have described.

Preconditions for Cognitive Growth

In 1964, Jean Piaget described four conditions which must exist if growth to formal thought is to occur. By attending to these conditions, we can teach in a way that will develop our students' thinking abilities.

1. Neural Maturation

The first condition, neural maturation, means that formal thought does not occur until a certain amount of maturity is reached by the brain. The maturation referred to is that which occurs in the neocortex of the brain. The neocortex is the thin outer layer of cells of the two hemispheres of the brain which makes up the majority (85 percent) of the brain's 3-pound mass. The massive number (tens of billions) of interconnected neurons process the thinking, reasoning, ideas, abstractions, and learned rational behavior that defines much of what is done by learners in schools.

Most of the neurons of the brain are in place within 18 months of birth. The development of the axon and dendrite branches accounts for the expansion of the brain from about 1 to 3 pounds. The genetic makeup of the individual will determine the establishment of the essential neural connections, and these rates vary widely among individuals.

Findings of Dr. Herman Epstein (1984) suggest that in about 85 percent of humans, this growth does not occur at a steady rate, but rather in a pattern of "spurts." Interestingly enough, these spurts seem to coincide approximately with the ages when the textbooks tell us that growth from one cognitive period to another is supposed to occur. Some researchers are suggesting that by introducing inappropriate content, we may be doing more than creating frustration—we may actually be creating negative neural networks. Whether we believe that the brain matures in stages or in regular patterns, the important idea is that in

Some researchers are suggesting that by introducing inappropriate content, we may be doing more than creating frustration— we may actually be creating negative neural networks.

any educational setting dealing with students up to 20 years old, these neural branches are present in some students and not yet in others. This is not to say that this maturation will not occur; it is that it has not happened at this point. How can we blame a student for not understanding a concept which requires these branches if they are not present, but will appear later?

A second part of the scenario is related to what happens as the branches are being laid down and after they are present. Environmental circumstances will effect the nature of the specific connections so that as the maturation occurs, each brain is a unique result of the experiences undergone as the branches were developed.

Robert Sylvester (1986) writes,

> The basic developmental pattern is simple and straightforward: (1) create an initial excess of connections (axons/dendrites/synapses) among related areas (2) use learning and experience to strengthen the useful connections and then prune away the unused and inefficient, and (3) maintain enough synaptic flexibility to allow neural connections to shift about throughout life as conditions change and new learning/ problem solving challenges emerge. (p. 91)

The learning environment which we establish to provide the strengthening and flexibility are provided in the other three preconditions.

2. Concrete Experience

By definition, concrete thinkers can understand only that which they have directly experienced through the senses, and we must provide experiences which allow them to do that. As a case in point, we are often asked to assess the thinking of students in schools before working with the staff, and in some schools we encounter a situation which clearly illustrates the

16

Can you make the triangle of pennies point the other direction in only three moves?

importance of concrete experience. In some elementary schools, we find that there will be an identifiable group of students who are able to function at the concrete level while their classmates give preoperational responses. Teachers expect the more successful group to be the gifted students, but this is seldom the case. In fact, during these assessments, students from the learning disabilities classes almost always perform at the higher levels, and when the teachers see and are surprised by this situation, they invariably give us the same explanation. They tell us that the students in the learning disabilities classes are being provided with hands-on experiences while the rest of the students are not.

To put it as simply and directly as we know how, we believe that to the extent we have taken hands-on activities out of the classroom, we have denied our students the opportunity to understand the ideas we are trying to teach.

3. Social Transmission

When knowledge is acquired from another person, the acquisition occurs by social transmission. Social

To put it as simply and directly as we know how, we believe that to the extent we have taken hands-on activities out of the classroom, we have denied our students the opportunity to understand the ideas we are trying to teach.

17

Can you tell me what a peanut looks like?

transmission and social interaction are synonymous (Renner and Marek, 1988). Through communication (talking is the most common kind of transmission), intellectual development is taking place.

The act of verbalizing one's thinking to others is a critical part of the thinking, learning, and understanding process. As Robert Sternberg (1987) points out:

Traditionally, psychologists conceived of thought as something that originates inside the individual, and only then is expressed socially. Psychologists have recently come to realize the great extent to which thought emerges as a social process and is internalized only after it has been socially expressed. (p. 458)

Cooperative learning groups are an excellent vehicle for social interaction and verbalizing thinking. There is something magical in the process of people (in this case, students) working on problems in small groups. Adults are not required in these groups, but they may be allowed if they follow some rules. The most important of these is that if an adult—a teacher, for example—is allowed in such a group, he or she must *not* provide answers, but must ask questions. Growth occurs as a result of students being out of equilibrium with a problem, and the purpose of a good question is just that: to create disequilibrium. When the understanding finally comes, it must happen inside the students' heads. No matter how tempting it is, if we tell the students the answer, we deny those students the opportunity to figure it out for themselves, and real understanding will not occur. Remember that when students are told the answer to a question, all thinking stops.

4. Equilibration

Equilibration is a grand term for a grand experience. It is that magic moment when the light finally dawns. "Aha!" is a term frequently used to describe it. It is the purpose of the entire exercise, and until it happens, understanding and growth have not happened. In order for an "Aha!" to happen, the person must first be put into a state of disequilibrium—that is, he or she must be puzzled or confused about something.

A friend of ours observes that "disequilibrium ain't pretty." In fact, it is uncomfortable. One of the reasons we tend to give students the answers, instead of letting them figure things out for themselves, is that it makes us uneasy to watch them struggle. On the other hand, when the "Aha!" happens, it is a wonderful experience. The real thinkers of the world are those who understand that they have to tolerate the discomfort of disequilibrium in order to achieve the satisfaction of equilibration. One of our jobs as teachers is to keep our students out of equilibrium as much as possible, not because we enjoy tormenting them, but because that is the only way for them to become comfortable with the disequilibrium-equilibration process.

To review, we have defined higher-level thinking skills as those skills which characterize formal thought. Specifically, they include, but are not limited to, theoretical reasoning, proportional reasoning, combinatorial reasoning, isolation and control of variables, probabilistic reasoning, and correlational reasoning. Students who possess these skills are able to understand and reason with complex and abstract concepts and ideas, both within and beyond their own experience, and can use symbolic language and abstract, concept-loaded words. We have also identified the preconditions for the development of formal thought as being neural maturation, concrete experience, social transmission, and equilibration. We have described equilibration as being the experience when true "understanding" actually occurs. Finally, we have defined "understanding" as being able to apply a concept, process, or idea to an entirely new situation. It seems clear, then, that the role of teachers must be to structure experiences for students which will lead them toward the moment of equilibration.

The Learning Cycle

An instructional model which, when implemented carefully in classrooms, helps students grow in their reasoning ability is commonly called a *learning cycle*. This model was originally developed by Robert Karplus and colleagues (1978) at the Lawrence Hall of Science at the University of California at Berkeley, and was first implemented in the Science Curriculum Improvement Study (SCIS). Several variations of this model exist (Lawson, 1988; Barman, 1989), and it continues to be the major instructional strategy in newly developed science curricula (e.g., the Biological Sciences Curriculum Study's [1989] new program, *Science for Life and Living*, and *Full Option Science System* [Center for Multisensory Learning Staff, 1990]). The format which we believe best lends itself to classroom implementation is described in the next four sections.

Asking an Interesting Question

An instructional activity should begin with a question or challenge. The purpose of this is to generate disequilibrium and/or challenge the brain in wondering about the idea.

Exploring the Concept

During this phase, students interact with new materials and ideas with a minimum of guidance; there is no expectation that they will master anything as an immediate result of their explorations. The purpose of the explorations is to increase their base of experience and to raise additional questions which create disequilibrium with respect to their previous understandings. This phase is based upon the "concrete experience" and "social transmission" preconditions described earlier.

If you only had one match and you entered a room to start a kerosene lamp, an oil heater, and a wood stove, which would you light first? Explain.

It should be noted that these very important exploratory experiences come *before* the vocabulary is introduced and the concepts are discussed; the exploration forms the basis upon which the concepts are invented.

Inventing the Concept

This is where we attempt to structure an "Aha!" experience for the students. Through class discussion, peer interactions, and the use of resource materials (including textbooks), the student will attempt to make sense of the ideas embedded in the concept and see the need to apply vocabulary to the situation.

Applying the Concept

Here, students apply what they have learned to new situations. Students who have "Aha!'d" will solidify and expand their understanding, and for those who have not yet grasped the idea, this is a further opportunity to do so. The teacher is able to observe the extent to which individual students have reached understanding. (This should give you a solid clue as to what we will say about accountability in the next chapter.)

The application phase is also important in that it gives students opportunities to tie the concept to its use in the real world. We consistently observe students finding new and creative ways to think about the concept during application activities.

STEP #5—POST-ASSESSMENT: ASSESS STUDENT UNDERSTANDING OF THE CONCEPT

The post-assessment process involves one or both of two processes:

- asking questions which assess the thinking skills, such as those used in the initial assessment, to determine whether the cognitive structure has been developed in the student; and/or

Remember that if students do not answer correctly, it is because the instruction was not effective, or the objective was not appropriate in the first place.

- asking questions which require the student to apply the specific concept you have taught to a new situation, to determine whether the student really understands the concept.

If the student demonstrates understanding of a concept which requires a specific skill, you may assume that he or she has mastered the skill as well as the concept. To reduce the effects of memory, it is important not to announce, "This is a test on (ratios or genetics or whatever concept you taught)." Rather, you should find an entirely new situation or problem which requires the use of the concept or process. As was the case with the initial assessment, it is important not to communicate to the students that you are judging them by their responses. Remember that if they do not answer correctly, it is because the instruction was not effective, or the objective was not appropriate in the first place.

Chapter Four

Issues Raised by the Model

THE PROBLEM WITH TEXTBOOKS

The learning cycle works because it is consistent with what we know about how learning takes place. It exemplifies what we mean by a focus on learning. It also has the virtue of demonstrating very clearly what is wrong with most commercial educational materials.

We choose and use commercial materials because they save us valuable time. They "cover" the material that we choose or are required to teach, and they do so in an organized way. Unfortunately, way down deep in our heart of hearts, we know that what the kids tell us about them is true. They may be colorful, relevant, readable, or whatever the latest sales gimmick is, but the truth is that they are *boring*. If you compare most of these materials to the learning cycle, you will see why. They are written for people who already understand the concepts, like teachers, rather than for people who do not, such as students. *Specifically, these materials skip the exploration phase and enter the learning cycle at the invention phase.* This has the

Until disequilibrium occurs, students quite accurately see themselves as being forced to memorize someone else's solutions to someone else's problems, and that is boring.

effect of trying to invent the concept for the students instead of helping them to invent it for themselves.

By now you have undoubtedly realized that this is the fundamental flaw in teaching Model #1 (see page 15), which also begins with a definition of the concept or a formula and follows with examples which "prove" that the definition is true or the formula is correct. Unfortunately, you cannot have understanding without equilibration, and you cannot have equilibration without first being out of equilibrium, and you cannot have disequilibrium without exploration. The brain will not try to solve a problem until it recognizes a problem exists. Once that happens, the motivation for working on the problem becomes intrinsic, and the

19

Which line is longer?

teacher no longer needs to beg, bribe, threaten, or cajole students into activity. Until disequilibrium occurs, however, the students quite accurately see themselves as being forced to memorize someone else's solutions to someone else's problems, and that is *boring*.

The fact that most texts aim for nothing more than memory-level understanding is made abundantly clear by the low-level verbs they use in their objectives. The following examples have been modified slightly from textbooks currently being used in schools. We would have loved to copy them exactly, and were more than willing to credit them appropriately, but it did not seem likely that we would be able to secure permission to do so.

Example I—Consider the following four objectives from a seventh-grade geography book:

1. *Give examples to show how the environment has influenced the way of life in the Woods Landing area.*

2. *List the ways technology has brought both benefits and problems to the people and industries in the Woods Landing area.*

3. *Locate and describe the geographical features and resources of the area.*

4. *Interpret and compare information shown in pictures, graphs, charts, and specialized maps.*

Notice that someone, consciously or unconsciously, has recognized that nonformal thinkers are not going to be able to understand the concepts included in objectives 1–3, so the operating words become "Give examples," "List," and "Locate and describe," which anyone with patience can memorize—and then forget. Objective #4 asks students to interpret and compare, which are formal activities that few seventh graders can do without learning cycle activities to help them understand.

Example II—Consider the thinking required for the task, "Using A Map Scale":

> *What is one of the first things you notice about any map? Everything has been drawn in a much smaller size than it really is. Each map must have a map scale. The map scale shows how many*

centimeters on the map stand for the number of kilometers on the land.

Each map has its own map scale. The maps on this page are about the same size, but you know that Woods Landing is not as big as Wyoming. The map scale on the Wyoming map tells you that 3 centimeters stand for 300 kilometers. How many kilometers are shown by 3 centimeters on the map of Woods Landing?

Do It Yourself

A map scale is used to measure distance. Find Woods Landing and Dull Center on the map of Wyoming. Use a ruler to measure the distance between those two cities. Now use the map scale to find out how far Dull Center is from Woods Landing.

True understanding of this activity requires proportional logic (A is to B as C is to D). This is a formal skill. This activity was modified from a book being used with fifth graders, almost none of whom are formal thinkers. This is why we commonly use "concrete crutches."

Example III—Consider the following objectives from a ninth-grade science book:

1. *Define "matter" and "energy."*

2. *Explain the difference between "mass" and "weight."*

3. *Give several examples of the "special properties" of matter.*

Notice the degree to which memorization is used to demonstrate "mastery" of the objective.

One of the major tasks confronting us as educators is the development of good learning cycle activities to use when teaching the concepts we have identified as important. The greatest need is in the area of exploratory activities. On the basis of our past experience with teachers, we are confident that once the development of these activities is perceived as a priority, they will be produced in great quantities.

How many ways can you turn a glassful of water upside down without spilling it?

To blame many of these problems on textbook publishers is fashionable, but remember that no one forces us to buy their books. In fact, the commercial materials which are consistent with the learning cycle have never sold well enough to justify keeping them in print. Many of the National Science Foundation materials are gathering dust in closets and storerooms, while the districts which own them spend money on new textbooks instead of in-service to find out how to use what they have. We recently learned (too late, alas) of a district auctioning off unopened sets of *Batteries and Bulbs* (The Elementary Science Study, 1968), one of the best learning cycle activities around.

A sales representative of a major textbook company recently described for us the features which teachers look for when texts are being considered for adoption:

One of the major tasks confronting us as educators is the development of good learning cycle activities to use when teaching the concepts we have identified as important.

1. the attractiveness of the illustrations, photographs, and artwork;

2. the usefulness of the teacher's guide; and

3. the presence of their favorite topics and the way these are presented.

A problem with these concerns is that different teachers have different favorite topics. To make certain that every teacher's favorite topic is included, the books have become huge and expensive. To make matters worse, some districts have taken the position that if it is in the book, it should be taught, with the result that teachers and kids are exhausting themselves trying to "cover" an entire textbook, when most of the material was only included in the book to improve sales.

Another example of the strange things that happen as a result of a focus on teaching instead of learning occurs in many of the very textbooks we just criticized for being inconsistent with the learning cycle. Many of them contain some very interesting activities, but instead of using them to introduce the concept and create disequilibrium, they are hidden at the back of the chapter in sections called something like "further explorations." Some of these texts could be very useful if the teacher were to begin with these explorations from the end of the chapter, then take scissors and cut out the definitions at the beginning.

THE PROBLEM WITH GRADES

In Assumption 5 at the beginning of Chapter 1, we pointed out that schools are organized in such a way as to impede the teaching of "thinking." It is around the issue of equilibration that one of the most serious of those problems comes to light. No matter what the teacher does, the "Aha!" may not happen according to schedule. It may not happen this period, or today, or this week, or this month, or even this year, yet we are required to give grades to the kids. We believe that the following dilemma is at the very heart of some of the craziness that goes on in schools:

Nonformal thinkers cannot understand formal concepts, but if we give them only concrete work to do, they will never grow. What this means in the real world of school is that teachers have two choices. We can give students work that they are not able to do, then flunk them for not doing it, or we can give them work which they are already able to do and watch them stagnate.

It may not be a conscious choice, but we suspect that most teachers are aware of this problem, choose the lesser of the two evils, and settle for memory-level activities.

Can you balance this quarter on the edge of this dollar bill?

To return to an earlier problem, if a student is working on an objective and cannot master it because the instruction wasn't effective, it is difficult for us to understand how this can be the student's fault. However, it is the student who gets the F. Likewise, if the student cannot master the objective because it is inappropriate, it is equally difficult for us to see how that can be his or her fault. But again, it is the student

Teachers have two choices. We can give students work that they are not able to do, then flunk them for not doing it, or we can give them work which they are already able to do and watch them stagnate.

who gets the F. We wish to make it clear that we do not believe it is the teacher's fault either. That good person is simply trying to survive in a system which forces him or her to flunk children or stifle them.

What about the kids who avoid working on the objective? We may just be playing semantic games, but it is hard for us to see how students can fail at something that they haven't even tried. Also, it is not at all surprising to us that children avoid working on objectives. If we were your students, and our experience in your class was one of continually being asked to solve problems and deal with questions which put us out of equilibrium, but that state of disequilibrium was encouraged (rather than punished), we might be frustrated from time to time, but we would learn to approach our tasks with some enthusiasm as we became more comfortable with the process.

22

Is the glass half full or half empty?

On the other hand, if you were to announce that you are going to give us work to do that may be too difficult for us because the process of struggling with the problems will cause us to grow intellectually, but you are going to flunk us if we don't have it done by the end of the period, we are going to fight you. If we are the so-called "good kids," we may just fight you by memorizing our way around your tests, but we might also cheat, raise Cain in your classroom, or withdraw, either literally or by not doing our work. One way or another, we are going to divert attention away from our inability to do your assignments.

While we recognize that the state of disequilibrium is not altogether comfortable, we suspect that most of you would agree it is preferable to the boredom of memorization. At times memorizing is necessary, but even then it can be a deadly, tedious, unpleasant business. Disequilibrium is preferable, but not if one is going to be punished for not getting out of that state on a schedule established by the teacher.

We already know about the arguments that doing away with grades cannot be done because the parents will not allow it or the board of education or administration will not allow it, and we already know about the argument that grades are good motivators. We don't buy those arguments for two reasons. First, it should be clear that not only do grades make no sense, but they are actually destructive to the process. Second, there are acceptable alternatives. Many alternative strategies, such as portfolios, performance measures, and process measures, are available. The first thing to do is make absolutely sure that the reluctance to abandon grades is not really fear of losing teachers' control over students, or the perfectly natural fear of wandering off into the unknown. If the former fear is present, realize that students who are out of equilibrium with a problem have a natural inclination to resolve that disequilibrium. If the classroom environment is one which encourages and supports this process, students will work on these problems willingly, out of a sense of intrinsic motivation, and the need for control will not be so strong. If the latter fear is present, we suggest that you give yourself permission to

While we recognize that the state of disequilibrium is not altogether comfortable, we suspect that most of you would agree it is preferable to the boredom of memorization.

understand that this is a perfectly normal reaction, and reduce the size and scale of the problem to something more manageable and less scary. Two districts with which we have recently worked have adopted a strategy which we think makes considerable sense. Their position is as follows:

1. Teaching kids to think is important, and we are going to do it.

2. We understand that giving grades is counterproductive to this process.

3. Giving up grades is scary.

4. Our long-range goal is to incorporate the teaching of thinking skills into every possible part of teaching.

5. Number 4 is also scary, because we have a lot to learn before we get there.

   THEREFORE: We propose to set aside at least one small portion of each day to begin with, and devote that time to thinking. We will not give grades during that portion of the day, but will concentrate on becoming more skilled at what we are doing, including listening to our students so as to do a better job of evaluating what they can and cannot do. Later, as we become better at it, we will increase the amount of time we devote to thinking skills. WE WANT EVERYONE IN OUR SCHOOL TO GET *FRIENDLY* WITH THINKING!

Another approach which appears to have merit is to give grades, but to base them upon contracts which specify what the students will do rather than what they will learn. This separates the grade from the learning, which is as it should be.

When we insist on abandoning grades for thinking activities, we are *not* suggesting that we abandon accountability. Our point is simply that grades get in the way of process and provide no honest accountability anyway. There is no good reason to keep them and there are good reasons to get rid of them.

ACCOUNTABILITY

We have not been bashful about our belief that grades are an abomination which have no place in a legitimate educational process. The fact remains that you, your students, administrators, and parents need and deserve accurate information about what your students are learning. If you think about it, the information we have provided gives not only a model for instruction, but the ability to report what students are learning with far greater accuracy than any grading system we have seen. The way students respond to these activities provides us with the information we need to know about how they think about the concepts, processes, and questions involved.

23

How many sides does a lead pencil have?

This information helps us to plan, but it also allows us to report on student progress. For example, if you were a second-grade teacher, would you rather be told that a student got a D in first-grade math, or that the student is a nonconserver of numbers? The D tells you nothing of value, but the information about the student's inability to conserve tells you exactly what you need to know to plan appropriate instruction and explain to administrators and parents why you are doing what you are doing.

Consider the learning environments that the implementation of this model could generate. Imagine a classroom where, through the use of learning centers, hands-on activities, and person-to-person interactions involving challenging questions, the students were engaged in activities which would allow us to assess their levels of reasoning. Some children would look at the two pieces of clay and say, "The pancake has more clay." Others would say, "Why are you asking me that dumb question? Of course they are the same." Still others might look at the two pieces curiously, scratch their heads, change the shapes, and place them on the balance. They might also discuss their observations with other children and through these processes develop the structure of the conservation of substance.

24

Am I putting the box down or picking it up?

Accountability is just that—collecting and reporting useful information about the intellectual growth of students.

This learning environment—where students interact with a small piece of information, are asked an interesting question about it, and respond from their own perspectives without fear of "being wrong" or not having the "right answers"—has great potential to provide information about the growth of the students, once we become skilled at collecting and reporting. It seems to us that accountability is just that—collecting and reporting useful information about the intellectual growth of students.

RELATIONSHIP TO SOME OTHER THEORIES OF LEARNING

We are frequently asked about the relationship of the model we have proposed to other educational models, especially behaviorism, mastery learning, and Bloom's *Taxonomy of Educational Objectives* (1956). We believe, of course, that our model incorporates the strengths of each of these models, while avoiding some of the pitfalls. Our intent is not to suggest that there is only one way to teach. Rather, it is to provide information that can be used to determine when and how different instructional strategies or materials can be effectively used as part of your educational program. It has been helpful to us to distinguish among behavior modification, behaviorism, mastery learning, diagnostic and prescriptive approaches to learning, Bloom's *Taxonomy of Educational Objectives,* and cooperative learning.

Behavior Modification

The important thing to remember about behavior modification is that it has nothing whatsoever to do

The important thing
to remember
about behavior
modification is that
it has nothing
whatsoever to do
with thinking or
understanding.

25

Without looking, can you draw where the numbers and letters go on a Touch-Tone® phone?

with thinking or understanding. Eugene Howard (1978) has observed that the effects of behavior modification are to increase students' dependence upon teachers and teach them to learn for the wrong reasons. However, it is a useful technique for controlling student behavior so that other things may take place, and such measures are required in certain situations. If we see a small child run into the street, our reaction is going to be to apply some immediate and powerful negative reinforcement. We do not suspect for a minute that, as the result of our disciplining, the child will understand that streets are dangerous places because of vehicles. There is time for that later. The exploration phase may be critical to the success of the learning cycle, but it is not the way for small children to learn about certain aspects of the world, such as the dangers of streets and moving vehicles.

Behaviorism

This is a more generalized approach, characterized by a total focus on the observation and measurement of behavior as an indicator of mastery. It is a very useful process for teaching skills, such as tying shoes or changing a tire or turning on a computer. For this type of teaching, which is probably more accurately described as training, behavioral approaches are more efficient, and in many cases more desirable, than the learning cycle. As with the child and the street, we are delighted that people do not learn to drive cars or fly airplanes using the learning cycle.

One problem with behaviorism is that there are limits as to what can be evaluated on the basis of behavior. What people do may not be an accurate reflection of what they are thinking, feeling, or believing. For example, if you are a woman and you work for a man who treats you with scrupulous attention to equity, we are sure you already know that you cannot assume he wouldn't really prefer that you were at home fixing someone's dinner. It is entirely possible that his behavior has been modified by the courts and edicts from his superiors. Again, in defense of behaviorism and behavior modification, this situation is clearly preferable to what would happen if he could behave as he wished, but it is also different from you being treated fairly because he respects you as a person.

To look at the situation from an educational perspective:

> Let us take as an example the quantification of class inclusion. No behaviorist can explain why all children begin by saying that there are more dogs than animals. Neither can behaviorists explain why, without any teaching whatsoever, children later come to say that there are more animals than dogs. Furthermore, in the quantification of class inclusion, there is no extinction. Once the child believes that there are more animals than dogs, there is no convincing him that he should go back to his previous belief. (Kamii, 1981, p. 232)

79

The instructional models recommended by many mastery learning programs do not follow the learning cycle. As a result, it is not likely that any thinking will occur or that any understanding will be achieved.

As teachers, we are interested in behavior, but we are, or we should be, more interested in thinking and understanding. We cannot continue to kid ourselves into thinking that we have taught children anything of value when they are only able to "list three causes of the American Revolution" or "define entropy." We must provide them with skills and understandings which will allow them to solve problems whenever and wherever they are encountered, be they in our classes or later in life. The behaviors we are looking for are the ability to apply thinking skills to new situations and an obvious pleasure in learning.

Mastery Learning

Mastery learning programs tend to be structured approaches designed to translate the philosophy of behaviorism into a workable teaching strategy. The approach we are advocating differs from mastery learning in at least three significant ways:

1. The mastery programs we have seen in schools define *mastery* as being able to pass a test, or an item on a test, rather than seeking the development of the kind of understanding which allows a child to apply his or her understanding in unfamiliar situations.

2. These programs often devote themselves exclusively to improving instruction without asking whether the objective was appropriate in the first place. Please recall our problem regarding the alternatives when a student is unable to "master" an objective. (See page 12.)

3. The instructional models recommended by many mastery learning programs do not follow

81

the learning cycle. There is no exploration phase, no attempt to create disequilibrium, and no guarantee of either concrete experience or social transmission. As a result, it is not likely that any thinking will occur or that any understanding will be achieved. Their value is that in every school, a large body of factual material, such as multiplication tables, safety rules, and mnemonics for spelling rules (e.g., "*i* before *e* except after *c*") must be memorized. For this type of material, mastery learning programs are more efficient, and in some cases, such as lab safety or driver training, much more desirable. However, if a logical concept must be understood before it can be applied, such as the concepts of number, subtraction, density, capitalism, nationalism, allegory, analogy, etc., the mastery model will not do the job, and the learning cycle approach is needed.

The Diagnostic and Prescriptive Approach

The diagnostic and prescriptive approach is characterized by the systematic development and implementation of instruction. It is based upon careful analysis of student abilities and limitations, followed by assessment of the effectiveness of the instruction. Planning based upon the results of the assessment follows. Model #2, which involves assessing the reasoning level of a student, then using a learning cycle to help the student understand the desired concept, is in fact a diagnostic and prescriptive approach. We first learned of the diagnostic and prescriptive approach from special educators; it is unfortunate that educators of non-handicapped students have tended to overlook the value of this approach, and it is equally regrettable that it has not been used to develop formal thinking in all students of all abilities.

Bloom's *Taxonomy*

As far as Bloom's *Taxonomy of Educational Objectives* (1956) is concerned, it seems to us that, as with behaviorism, there are problems with the way the model has been used. It is logical and useful, but many educators have forgotten to apply a developmental perspective. Remember that even in stimulating learning environments, students at the various levels (preoperational, concrete, and formal) will synthesize and evaluate in ways that are qualitatively different. For example, a nonconserver of mass will evaluate the available evidence in the clay ball activity described previously and conclude that the pancake weighs more. No matter which instructional techniques the teacher employs, the student will not believe that the two pieces of clay weigh the same until the structure of conservation is developed. A major part of our job as teachers is to remember that for the nonconserving student, this is a valid and appropriate answer at the higher levels of the taxonomy.

26

Why does cement get darker when you squirt water on it?

83

Cooperative Learning

Social transmission is a prerequisite for cognitive growth, and one of the many virtues of cooperative learning (Johnson, Johnson, and Johnson Holubec, 1988) is that it ensures that social transmission occurs in the classroom. To see the power of cooperative learning in this regard, all one needs to do is to count the number of times individual students express their thinking in a class which is using cooperative learning and compare it to the number of times they express their thinking in classes using other more didactic instructional strategies.

A FOOTNOTE ON ENTHUSIASM

27

Why is ¼ bigger than ⅕ when 4 is smaller than 5?

Finally, a bit more about our continued insistence that students approach these tasks with enthusiasm. This may appear to be a secondary consideration to someone who is dealing with 35 children in a class and a curriculum that increases in size every year. In fact, we are convinced that this may be the most important consideration of all. A friend of ours points out that because we care about what happens to kids, we tend to believe that the time they spend in our classroom is the most important time of all, because that is the only time we have to teach them all the wonderful things we know. If you stop and think about it, however, the most important time of all is the time after they finish school. If, in our haste to "cover" all of the material in the curriculum, we force them to deal with objectives and concepts which are not appropriate, penalize them for not understanding them, and bore them with an endless program of memorization, what we are likely to guarantee is that once they are through with school, they will go to great lengths to avoid ever dealing with anything resembling our subjects again. Our understanding of the American system of government is that it is based upon an informed electorate. If we have succeeded in causing people to avoid thinking about the historical, social, and scientific ideas required to understand today's issues, and have not developed in them the ability to understand complex and abstract ideas and problems, it is hard to see how any informed electorate is possible. Only about 50 percent of the adult population reaches the level of formal thought, and of this 50 percent most only think in a formal way about ideas and concepts which are associated with their occupations. Given the fact that only one-half of the adult population is capable of formal thought, is it surprising that so few people vote? (Question: Which half votes?)

A LEARNING CYCLE FOR TEACHERS

Practicing what we preach in this document is difficult when we are not with you to provide activities and ask questions. In spite of that, we propose to leave you with a learning cycle activity which deals with the concepts we have discussed.

1. *Asking questions and exploring:* Each of you has accumulated a tremendous body of concrete exploratory experience by virtue of your day-to-day interactions with students in the classroom. We have provided some questions which may prove disequilibrating to you. For example, who gets the F when a student fails to understand because of ineffective instruction or inappropriate objectives? Another is the question of what a teacher does when the only choices available are to (a) give students work that they cannot do and then flunk them for not doing it, or (b) stifle them with tasks they have already mastered. Another one which fascinates us is this: If the central purpose of education is to teach kids to think, why is it necessary for us to go to such lengths to justify using a small portion of the school day for thinking skills? Skim back through this book and highlight issues we raised that caused some disequilibrium for you.

2. *Inventing:* For the invention phase, we encourage you to do two things. First, conduct some assessment activities with your own students, so as to collect information on their cognitive development. Then analyze your curriculum, instructional activities, labs, and tests to see if they require understanding which is beyond your students' ability. Relate your findings back to the issues that caused disequilibrium for you.

3. *Applying:* Identify one of the concepts you have just analyzed, and find or invent some learning cycle activities which deal with that concept. Remember that if the concept is formal and your students have not yet developed formal thought, there is no harm in having them

engage in concrete exploration related to the concept, so long as you do not expect them to do any more than explore. Do not look for closure or understanding. Just remember that these experiences will help them to achieve understanding when they are ready, and that without experiences such as these, they may never reach that point.

CONCLUSIONS

It is possible at this point that you do not feel you are an expert at teaching kids how to think. That is O.K. We never expected that a document such as this would have that effect. We will be pleased indeed if as a result of reading this book, you have some questions about what is happening in schools at the present and some ideas about what to do in the future. The subject is a difficult one, and although the two of us have devoted 30 years to thinking about it and working on it, we are continually amazed at how little we know and fascinated by how much remains to be done. Don't be discouraged by that fact, because even though we have spent thousands of hours talking, arguing, and working on the problem, we have enjoyed every one of them.

If you decide to set off on this adventure, know that it is a long one, but that you will enjoy the trip. As a practical matter, we would encourage you to find a traveling companion. The road can get lonely when you are on it by yourself, and a partner not only helps with the loneliness, but provides the "social transmission" that makes the trip easier and more productive. If you have questions, please contact us. We enjoy very few things in this world more than discussing these questions with concerned educators. (Page 100 of the

"Selected Resources" section has information about how to contact us for upcoming workshops. The other resources listed on pages 97 to 99 will also provide valuable information for your trip.

Postscript

Quincy the Question Mark

If we are interested in establishing a learning environment where equilibration is happening and students are enjoying it, we must all be comfortable with questions like Quincy is asking. We and our students should look upon these types of questions and puzzles as challenges to be tackled with enthusiasm rather than threats to avoid.

If you decide to ask some of these questions in your classroom, do not judge or grade the students according to how quickly or easily they arrive at the answers. An "Aha!" that takes a long time to happen is just as valid and important to the learner as one that comes quickly. None of us is comfortable with disequilibration the first few times it happens or if we have not been involved with it in a long time. It takes considerable practice and persistence to look upon it as an exciting, rather than threatening, experience.

These words are just about as important for teachers as they are for students. If you present your students with some of Quincy's questions and leave them alone to work on the answers, get ready for them to turn the tables on you. Some of them will immediately go to the library or home to find some of these questions to ask you. If this threatens you, your students will sense it immediately, and so much for thinking skills with that group. Many of us haven't done much thinking lately. Let's accept this fact and have fun stretching our minds with the kids.

The answers to Quincy's questions appear below. As you read them, think about how boring they become. If you know any good questions for Quincy to ask, send them to us. Don't send the answers.

1. You don't hear the ocean; you hear the sound of air movement around the inside of the shell and of the movement of your hand on the shell. The sound is magnified by having the opening of the shell near your ear. Cup your hands and hold them near your ear. You will hear the same thing.

2. The boy's mother's father is only six years older than his father.

3. The snow lying on the ground, bushes, and trees provides fewer surfaces that reflect sound. Therefore, many of the sounds are absorbed and not heard.

4. When air is heated, the molecules do rise, but the rising effect also causes an expansion of the air. The expansion of a gas is a cooling process. Put your hand near the valve stem of a tire while air is escaping from it. The air is expanding and feels cool.

5. The air close to the hot road ahead is also hot, more of the molecules have risen, and thus it is less dense than the air just above it. This difference in density causes the light rays to bend just as they do when they travel through glass or water. When the bending effect is just right,

you see a mirage. You can actually take a picture of this one.

6. Don't let your thinking be restricted here. We didn't say that the glasses are glued down or that we can't pick them up. Pick up the second glass and pour the liquid from it into the fifth one.

7. 99 + %

8. When substances evaporate, the process draws heat from the surroundings, causing them to cool. Another example is the evaporation of freon in the coils of a refrigerator, which draws heat from the food inside.

9. If they are survivors, you don't really want to bury them, do you?

10. Noah is the person who took the animals on the Ark.

11. The bathroom scale uses a spring to measure how hard gravity is pulling your body to the earth. The spring will compress the same amount with one foot on the platform of the scale as with two. Try it.

12. Measure them; they are the same.

13. Use your own words. Invent new ones.

14. F, G, H; D, A, E, A, F; P, S, V (leave out two letters of the alphabet); S, S, E, N (first letters of the numbers); F, S, S (first letters of the days of the week); M, J, J (first letters of the months).

15. No. The volume of the box is measured by multiplying the vertical height of the box times the length and the width. The vertical height has decreased.

16. This is most easily done by drawing the pennies before and after the move.

17. Use your own words. Invent new ones if needed.

18. You should light the match first.

19. Both the lines are the same. Measure them.

20. Freeze it. Place it in a sink full of water and turn it upside down while it is submerged. Hold it at your side and whirl your arm around rapidly. You list some more.

21. Fold the dollar bill like an accordion and stand it on its edge. Put the quarter on the edge.

22. What do you think?

23. Count them.

24. What do you think?

25. Look at one.

26. If you look at the surface of cement under magnification, you will notice that it is rough. This rough surface reflects light in all directions like an ice cube that has been rubbed with sandpaper, giving the surface a light color. A thin film of water acts as a mirror on the surface and reflects the light rays more regularly. Fewer of them reach your eye, causing the surface to appear darker.

27. Would you rather have $\frac{1}{4}$ or $\frac{1}{5}$ of $1,000?

References

Arlin, P. (1984). *The Arlin test of formal reasoning.* Aurora, NY: Slosson Educational Publications.

Barman, C. (1989). *An expanded view of the learning cycle: New ideas about an effective teaching strategy.* Washington, DC: Council of Elementary Science International Monograph, 4.

Biological Sciences Curriculum Study. (1989). *Science for life and living: Integrating science, technology, and health.* Dubuque, IA: Kendall/Hunt Publishing.

Bloom, B. (Ed.). (1956). Taxonomy of educational objectives: The classification of educational goals. *Handbook I: Cognitive domain.* New York: Longman, Inc.

Center for Multisensory Learning Staff at Lawrence Hall of Science, University of California—Berkeley. (1990). *Full option science system.* Chicago, IL: Encyclopaedia Britannica Educational Corporation.

Copeland, R. (1988). *Piagetian activities: A diagnostic and developmental approach.* Eau Claire, WI: Thinking Publications.

Educational Policies Commission. (1963). *Schools for the 60s.* New York: McGraw Hill.

The Elementary Science Study. (1968). *Batteries and bulbs.* New York: McGraw Hill, Webster Division.

Ellsworth, P., and Sindt, V. (1991). *The classroom assessment of student reasoning.* Loveland, CO: L & L Distributing.

Epstein, H. (1979). Cognitive growth and development: Brain growth and cognitive functions. *Colorado Journal of Educational Research, 19*(1), 4–5.

Epstein, H. (1984). Brain growth and cognitive development: A response to Richard McQueen. *Educational Leadership, 41*(5), 72–75.

Goodlad, J. (1984). *A place called school.* New York: McGraw Hill.

Howard, E. (1978). *School discipline handbook.* New York: Parker.

Johnson, D., Johnson, R., and Johnson Holubec, E. (1988). *Cooperation in the classroom.* Edina, MN: Interaction Book Company.

Kamii, C. (1981). Applications of Piaget's theory to education—the preoperational level. In I. Sigel, D. Brodzinsky, and R. Golnikoff (Eds.), *New directions in Piagetian theory and practice.* Hillsdale, NJ: Lawrence Erlbaum Associates.

Karplus, R., Lawson, A., Wollman, W., Appel, M., Bernhoff, R., Howe, A., Rusch, J., and Sullivan, F. (1978). *Science teaching and development of reasoning.* Berkeley, CA: Lawrence Hall of Science, University of California at Berkeley.

Lawson, A. (1988). *Three types of learning cycles: A better way to teach science.* Paper presented at the annual convention of the National Association for Research in Science Teaching, Lake Ozark, MO.

Madden, R., Gardner, E., Rudman, H., Karlsen, B., and Merwin, J. (1973). *Stanford achievement test.* New York: Harcourt, Brace, Jovanovich.

Marzano, R., Brandt, R., Hughes, C., Jones, B., Rankin, S., and Suhor, C. (1988). *Dimensions of thinking: A framework for curriculum and instruction.* Alexandria, VA: Association for Supervision and Curriculum Development.

Mullis, I., Dossey, J., Owen, E., and Phillips, G. (1991). *The state of mathematics achievement: Executive summary.* Princeton, NJ: Educational Testing Service.

Mullis, I., and Jenkins, L. (1988). *The science report card: Elements of risk and recovery.* Princeton, NJ: Educational Testing Service.

Mullis, I., Owen, E., and Phillips, G. (1990). *America's challenge: Accelerating academic achievement. A summary of findings from 20 years of NAEP.* Princeton, NJ: Educational Testing Service.

National Commission on Excellence in Education. (1983, April 27). An open letter to the American people. A nation at risk: The imperative for educational reform. *Education Week,* pp. 12–16.

Piaget, J. (1964). Cognitive development in children: Development and learning. *Journal of Research in Science Teaching, 2,* 176–186.

Renner, J., and Marek, E. (1988). *The learning cycle and elementary school science teaching.* Portsmouth, NH: Heinemann Educational Books.

Shepard, L. (1989). Why we need better assessments. *Educational Leadership, 46*(7), 5–6.

Sigel, I., and Cocking, R. (1977). *Cognitive development from childhood to adolescence: A constructivist perspective.* New York: Holt, Rinehart, and Winston.

Sternberg, R. (1987). Teaching critical thinking: Eight easy ways to fail before you begin. *Phi Delta Kappan, 68*(6), 456–459.

Sylvester, R. (1986). Synthesis of research on brain plasticity: The classroom environment and curriculum enrichment. *Educational Leadership, 44*(1), 90–93.

United States Forest Service. (1972). *Environmental education for teachers and research people.* Washington, DC: U.S. Department of Agriculture.

Worsham, A., and Austin, G. (1983). Effects of teaching thinking skills on SAT scores. *Educational Leadership, 40,* 50–51.

Selected Resources

BOOKS

Baratta-Lorton, M. (1976). *Mathematics their way.* Menlo Park, CA: Addison Wesley.

Baratta-Lorton, M. (1976). *Workjobs.* Menlo Park, CA: Addison Wesley.

Barman, C., Johnson, V., Leyden, M., and Rusch, J. (1982). *Teaching science—grades 5–9.* Dallas, TX: Silver Burdett.

Bybee, R., and Sund, R. (1982). *Piaget for educators* (2nd ed.). Columbus, OH: Charles E. Merrill.

Copeland, R. (1988). *Piagetian activities: A diagnostic and developmental approach.* Eau Claire, WI: Thinking Publications.

Copple, C., Sigel, I., and Saunders, R. (1979). *Educating the young thinker: Classroom strategies for cognitive growth.* New York: D. Van Nostrand and Company.

Donalson, M. (1978). *Children's minds.* New York: W.W. Norton and Company.

Duckworth, E. (1987). *"The having of wonderful ideas" and other essays on teaching and learning.* New York: Teachers College Press.

Educational Policies Commission. (1961). *The central purpose of American education.* Washington, DC: National Education Association.

Elkind, D. (1981). *The hurried child: Growing up too fast too soon.* Reading, MA: Addison Wesley.

Elkind, D. (1988). *Miseducation: Preschoolers at risk.* New York: Alfred Knopf.

Ellsworth, P., and Sindt, V. (1987). *Starpath.* Laramie, WY: Woods Landing Institute.

Furth, H., and Wachs, H. (1974). *Thinking goes to school.* New York: Oxford University Press.

Hendrickson, A. (1979). *Math the Piaget way.* St. Paul, MN: Department of Education.

Hyde, A., and Bizar, M. (1989). *Thinking in context.* New York: Longman.

Iozzi, L., and Bastardo, P. (1983). *Preparing for tomorrow's world.* Longmont, CO: Sopris West, Inc.

Joyce, B., and Weil, M. (1986). *Models of teaching.* Englewood Cliffs, NJ: Prentice Hall, Inc.

Karplus, R., Lawson, A., Wollman, W., Appel, M., Bernhoff, R., Howe, A., Rusch, J., and Sullivan, F. (1978). *Science teaching and development of reasoning.* Berkeley, CA: University of California at Berkeley.

Lowrey, L. (1989). *Thinking and learning.* Pacific Grove, CA: Midwest Publications.

Renner, J., and Marek, E. (1988). *The learning cycle and elementary school science teaching.* Portsmouth, NH: Heinemann Educational Books.

Rozenzweig, L. (Ed.). (1982). *Developmental perspectives in the social studies.* Washington, DC: National Council of Social Studies.

Ryan, F. (1980). *The social studies sourcebook.* Boston, MA: Allyn and Bacon.

Shayer, M., and Adey, P. (1981). *Towards a science of science teaching.* London: Heinemann.

Sigel, I., Brodzinsky, D., and Golnikoff, R. (1981). *New directions in Piagetian theory and practice.* Hillsdale, NJ: Lawrence Erlbaum and Associates.

Sigel, I., and Cocking, R. (1977). *Cognitive development from childhood to adolescence: A constructivist perspective.* New York: Holt, Rinehart, and Winston.

Singer, D., and Revenson, T. (1978). *How a child thinks.* New York: Plume.

Wadsworth, B. (1978). *Piaget for the classroom teacher.* New York: Longman.

Waller, T. (1977). *Think first, read later.* Newark, NJ: International Reading Association.

ARTICLES

Epstein, H. (1984). Brain growth and cognitive development: A response to Richard McQueen. *Educational Leadership, 41*(5), 72–75.

Johnson, V. (1982). Myelin and maturation: A fresh look at Piaget. *The Science Teacher, 49*(3), 41–44, 49.

Kamii, C. (1984). Autonomy: The aim of education envisioned by Piaget. *Phi Delta Kappan, 65*(6), 410–415.

Lawson, A. (1978). Classroom test of formal reasoning. *Journal of Research in Science Teaching, 15,* 11–24.

McQueen, R. (1984). Spurts and plateaus in brain growth: A critique of the claims of Herman Epstein. *Educational Leadership, 41*(5), 67–71.

Worsham, A., and Austin, G. (1983). Effects of teaching thinking skills on SAT scores. *Educational Leadership, 41*(3), 50–51.

WORKSHOPS

For information on upcoming workshops, please call Peter Ellsworth or Vincent Sindt at 307-742-4388, or write to them at 2474 Jefferson St., Laramie, WY 82070.